Physical Resource Management

Philip Sanders

Physical Resource Management, 1st Edition

Published by Skybow Group – Idaho Falls, Idaho 83404

ISBN: 978-0-578-04815-4

Dedication

This book is dedicated to the people that work in the physical resource management field, those that have gone before, blazing the trail, and those that do this work now and in the future.

An associate of mine in the physical resource management field has a favorite saying about our work; "there is no glory in it". She says this because often the work is hard and the only time some people show they care is when things go wrong.

That is why this book is dedicated to the people in the field.

Acknowledgments

Thanks to family and friends that were patient with me and helped in many ways.

I appreciate the outstanding editing from First Editing.

The cover was designed by Mark Paulsen, my friend and brother in the Lord.

Forward

My vision for this work is to create a guide for both executives that have management responsibility for and the practitioners
of the various facets of physical resource management. The book
is succinct to meet the needs of both of these audiences.

My ideal for this work was <u>The One Minute Manager</u>, a
great book that is also succinct, yet powerful and enduring.

Table of Contents

CHAPTER 1 - HIGHLIGHTS

- **Physical Resource Management**

- **Purpose**

- **PRM System**

This book provides an overview of the discipline of physical resource management. Physical resource management has many facets and is considered an important activity by most businesses. The activities that comprise the current discipline of physical resource management have titles that vary widely within organizations. The field covers work ranging from commercial and residential real estate activities to controlling the physical resources of companies and government agencies.

Today the work of these activities is organized in many different ways and in a variety of entities (companies, nongovernmental organizations, non-profit institutions, and local, state, and national governments). Entities that have a large investment in physical resources must expend necessary energy and resources to manage their physical resources to benefit the company owners, stockholders and stakeholders. In the case of most governments, this effort is necessary to benefit the citizens or taxpayers; in most government types, the citizens actually own the physical resources.

Physical resource management (which will be referred to by the acronym PRM throughout this work) processes have developed in an undisciplined way over time and that is part of the imperative for PRM in the 21st century. Implementation of an effective and efficient PRM system can reduce costs in several organizational units that currently perform some PRM processes in less than efficient ways. Specific examples of this are project management, accounting, and procurement activities that perform the work as sort of a sideline to their core work. When such organizations perform PRM work, it is often, and understandably, sub-optimized with respect to their core missions.

When an entity implements an effective PRM system, parts of this work performed across the enterprise can be made more efficient and effective, thereby reducing the costs of performing this work. PRM provides value by leveraging physical resources (which will be referred to by the acronym PR throughout this work) to ensure and enable completion of the mission of entities.

This book is one of the first to describe how all of these work areas are inter-related in the broader context of Physical Resource Management.

This work defines Physical Resource Management as:

The systematic identification and control of physical resources.

And defines the Physical Resource Management System (PRMS) as:

> ## *The procedures, processes, and tools used for life cycle management of physical resources.*

The primary thrust of PRM is the same as many other business processes: to increase value to the organization and the shareholders and or stakeholders. The secondary thrust of PRM is to reduce risks to the enterprise arising from the ownership and or operation of Physical Resources. When an organization's PRM achieves these primary and secondary goals it will certainly produce products and services that align with the enterprise needs of internal customers and external clients.

This work strives to provide the executives that manage Physical Resources and the practitioners of the PRM discipline with knowledge for application. In addition, it is intended to serve as a reference that can be used throughout the working career of the reader.

CHAPTER 2 - HIGHLIGHTS

- ## PRM Description

- ## Key Categories

- ## Life Cycle Functions

Physical Resources must be managed to ensure a level of control that is vital to the financial success of the entity that owns the Physical Resources (PR). This is true because it is based on the presumption that the PR are needed to perform the mission of the entity; if the PR were not needed there would be no reason to have them. The system that is used to manage the PR should be proportional to the volume of PR to be controlled. Physical Resources managed. Two simple examples show the logic of proportionality.

The small business that is run out of a single office with a handful of employees might use a spreadsheet as part of the accounting system which contains all necessary information about the firms' PR. The data is likely simple, with a description and cost that is primarily used for documenting the depreciation expenses for tax purposes. But though it may be simple, all the elements of PRM would be covered in this simple process. It is very likely that all of the PR can be accounted for immediately and that all are considered necessary to the operation of the business.

On the other end of the spectrum, the General Services Administration is responsible for managing the PR of the United States Government. As of 2008, the PR of the Unites States consisted of millions of items with an accounting book value of over one trillion dollars. The GSA clearly must use more than a spreadsheet with a description and cost to manage these PR. It is also not very likely that all of these PR can be accounted for immediately and that all are effectively used and considered essential to the operation of the government.

These examples also point out two major distinct groups of PR that are managed by Physical Resource Management systems. In one case privately owned PR are being managed and in the other public PR are being managed. In the case of private PR there are two key types of PR, those held by private companies and those held by public companies. In the case of public PR, which are owned by the people of the country (in all types of government except maybe dictatorships), state or other government entity, there are two key divisions. Public PR are managed by the employees of the government or increasingly managed by companies that contract to do work for the government. All of these entities inherently do the work differently, but all do the work somehow, or they would not be able to perform their missions.

The types of PR that a PRM system is all about are generally categorized as fixed PR, consumable items, and finished goods for sale. There are several definitions that provide both descriptions and a categorization of items. These key categories are; 1) Real PR, 2) Equipment, 3) Raw material, 4) Supplies, and 5) Finished goods.

Real PR are generally real estate, buildings and other permanent fixtures such as electrical substations, sidewalks, parking lots, and other associated systems. There are specific needs relative to the PRM for real PR as these types of PR are much different than the other categories. This category of PR generally comprises the vast amount of the value of an entities physical asset value. The value of these PR also drives and justifies the resources that are allocated to management of these items.

Equipment is generally items that have a service life of some time, often a couple of years, and aren't consumed in use. These items are usually higher by volume than real PR, but lower in cost and value. The importance of these items is such that when managed well such PR can literally make or break an enterprise as they are vital to operations and mission success.

Raw materials are items bought that are used to manufacture other products either for use in operations or to produce finished goods to sell.

Supplies are spare parts and consumable items that include direct use (buy and use up) and or stocked and then used. The key to these items is that they are consumed in use in one of two ways. Some items are consumed and then become waste, e.g. a pencil. Other items are consumed in use as they lose their identity when installed into a higher level item. An example of this would be the engine in a vehicle, the vehicle is the equipment item and the engine is the consumable item. As you can imagine this item leveling can go up and down through several iterations, and determination of classifications is an important element of supply management. The management of these items through good supply management techniques is extremely vital to day to day operations of an enterprise.

Finished goods inventories, the products that an enterprise produces that are awaiting sale are also PR that are part of the PRM system.

The work of physical resource management is generally found in several areas of an organization. The organizational lash up for PR work often reflects the nature of the work of the enterprise in relation to how PR are categorized. Many of these functions are interfaces that most professional people are familiar with. The more commonly known areas are: PR Control, Equipment Management, Facility Operations, Inventory Control, PR Accounting, Material Management, Physical Distribution, Warehousing, and Logistics.

General definitions of these areas as elements of the PRM system vary widely and that is one of the compelling reasons for this work. Rather than define PRM organizationally, a life cycle functional definition should be used, and the organizational decisions and titles decided according the needs of the enterprise relative to the life cycle functions.

The five life cycle functional areas of PRM are:

1) Requirement Identification,

2) Acquisition,

3) Asset Identification,

4) Use and,

5) Disposal.

Definitions of these life cycle phases are described below.

The life cycle phase of requirements identification is of course the beginning of the PRM system. When the designer of something decides that an asset is needed, the requirement identification process begins. The key to successful PRM is that this phase includes multiple disciplines and a good decision is made about the asset. For example, the decision that a building is needed will result in a relatively large expenditure. When the PRM process starts in this phase, the overall life cycle costs of performing PRM are lower.

Acquisition of PR is usually done through the procurement processes of an organization. The key to effective PRM operations is visibility during this process so that life cycle management decisions about quantity, location, and usage parameters are well coordinated with users and managers of PR.

One overlooked aspect of the life cycle of PR is the asset identification element. In the traditional approach to PRM activities, continuing even today this work is part of an entities receiving function. Today this work does not always require a receiving function, rather the implementation of identification of items for PRMS using technology and communication techniques to effectively and efficiently perform these actions. This does not mean that receiving is an unnecessary process, only that a good receiving process is not the best solution, and when the identification function is removed from receiving the receipt activities are done more quickly and generally cost less. Good receiving processes will mitigate the risk of erroneous payments, payment for things not provided as specified in acquisition contracts, and damages to PR by third parties before receipt. Receiving processes also provide critical data for effective life cycle management processes.

Use of PR is the most critical life cycle element in the PRM system. The pre-computer age processes for implementing asset control resulted in many organizational conflicts that have persisted and ultimately cost enterprises much efficiency over time. Smart and efficient use of today's automated data processing tools in the PRM system offers the enterprise great opportunity for reduction of costs in both the asset life cycle and in operations. The use life cycle covers everything that happens to an asset after receipt and before disposal.

The disposal phase covers what happens to PR when they are no longer needed. This phase is very scalable, from throwing away the stub of a pencil or other used up items to selling items in order to recover some of the remaining value.

CHAPTER 3 - HIGHLIGHTS

- **Procedures**

- **Processes**

- **Tools**

Physical Resource Management Systems (which will be referred to by the acronym PRMS) add value by efficiently and effectively managing PR. The PRM system is not a computer system. The computer systems used to manage data and processes about PR are tools that are part of the PRM system. Management of PR is vital to companies and government agencies that own or control PR. When companies have PR that are part of their operations, effective management of PR is vital to their profitability and staying in business. Government agencies that are charged with controlling the PR that are owned by the citizens of the country must also effectively manage their PR to maintain a viable government.

PR that require management are generally categorized as fixed PR, consumable items, and finished goods inventories. In the field of PRMS this work provides several definitions of categories that provide both descriptions and a classification of items that facilitates more efficient management processes:

These key categories are;

1) Real Physical Resources,

2) Equipment,

3) Raw material,

4) Supplies, and

5) Finished goods.

Management of these PR involves the entire life cycle of an asset. Generally, the physical asset life cycle is: requirement identification, acquisition, receipt, use, and disposal. Organizations that recognize this life cycle and develop and execute processes to efficiently manage their PR provide a significant benefit to their stakeholders.

A PRM system consists of the procedures, processes, and tools used to identify and track PR.

- Procedures – Ensure standardized and repeatable processes
- Processes – Provide efficient and effective products and services
- Tools – Enable performance of efficient and effective processes

Organizations that make a specific commitment to address the management of their PR using a systematic approach ensure that risks to shareholder value are addressed and mitigated. Companies that control clients' PR that they use during performance of work under contract with the client also agree to create a financial risk for their organization, and the PRM processes that address proper control of these PR ensure that this risk is mitigated.

PRM processes mitigate the financial risks that PR present to the financial well being of the company. The financial risks include losses of value due to interruption of operations when necessary PR is not present when needed. Other financial risks include the liabilities associated with loss, damage, and destruction of PR. Commercial standards and government regulations are the driver for many of the aspects of PRM, but the key driver is to ensure continued value to the shareholder. The direct link to shareholder value is clear whether the PR are owned by the company, the government, or a client.

The PRM process addresses the key aspects of managing PR that create the biggest financial risk from owning or controlling the PR. The PRM processes that have been created to implement the function have been dramatically improved for over two decades by entities that use software products to enable PRM.

When effectively implemented, PRM systems produce value for shareholders. There are five key aspects of Physical Resource Management that will be described in this system section. This system description is discussed from the functional perspective, but is different from a practitioner approach so that executives and managers can better understand this discipline and employ strategies to achieve best use of PR. They can use this work to develop and implement systems and also to evaluate how their systems are working. Most PRM documents are produced from the functional perspective, making them hard to understand unless you are very familiar with the concepts of PRM. For executives and managers, whether they "own" the PRMS functions, or just interface with them there are key aspects that help to understand the management of PR.

The key executive aspects of PRM are:

1) Integration,

2) Cost,

3) Organization,

4) Products, and

5) Services.

Integration of PRMS

Integration of the PRMS is a vital element of effective asset management. Effective and efficient management of PR demands integration across the enterprise, especially focusing on operations and maintenance activities. In really comprehensive operational environments, such as government owned, contractor operated facilities management type contracts, or other large operations, such as building aircraft or other complex machines, the focus on integration expands to include virtually all organizational elements.

Other key functional integration areas are with procurement, accounting, and material management activities. These key interfaces must include some method of data integration. Preferably this is done with an integrated enterprise system, but it can be done through either manual referencing for smaller entities (although that is usually much more costly in the long run) or through database integration.

Cost of PRM

An important aspect of integration is the impact on PRM costs across the enterprise. When PRMS is integrated and functioning maturely it should be within a range that varies between .0075 and .01 of total costs. When PRM systems are mature and operating at peak efficiency the cost could be less than three quarters of one percent (.0075) of the total entity operational costs. This assertion regarding cost is based on performing the function using the key principles described in this book. These leading edge processes have been proven to reduce costs to less than .01 of total entity operating cost in the most intensive risk control environments.

Organization of PRM

The PRM function can be organized separately or with another department or it can be aligned in several organizations. A very effective approach that promises great functional efficiencies for the future is integration of PRM with logistics and supply chain activities. A critical consideration is that the manager or leader of the PRMS functions must have access to top management when added horsepower is needed. The first key decision whether or not the function will be stand alone or part of another unit. Once the decision is made the leader of the organization must be empowered to develop and implement an effective PRM system. When properly organized, the outcome is based on good old fashioned management. There is one concept that is key to managing the PRM: establish accountability to be sure that the assigned leader develops and implements a PRM system that provides value and reduced risk.

PRM Products

For many involved with PRM it may seem a little out of place to discuss production in the PRM discipline, but it is a crucial discriminator for the leading edge system. PRM systems that are functioning at high levels produce six key products: 1) Lower asset costs, 2) Asset information for improved performance in operations & maintenance, 3) Reduced financial risk, 4) Documented processes, usually procedures, 5) Records of PR, and 6) Audit trails of transactions. These products are provided to operations and maintenance organizations so that they can use PR in the most productive way for their work. In the modern world these products are also critical to both internal company and external customers as primary outputs of the system.

Lower costs for PR across the enterprise result from the need to acquire lower volumes of PR to perform work. When no PRM system is present organizations must acquire more items to perform the same amount of work because the presence of like items is not known and duplicate items are acquired instead of using the complete capacity of existing items.

PRM Services

PRMS produces physical asset information products including basic things, such as total volume of items to reduce acquisition costs as noted above, and additional information items that are critical to operations and maintenance achieving the zenith of efficiency and effectiveness. In addition to asset volume information items, such as type, location, and availability for other uses, when provided to users facilitates their processes' efficiency and effectiveness.

Reduced financial risk for the entire entity results from the lower costs and improved efficiency and effectiveness of operations and maintenance and through delivery of value to stockholders and stakeholders of the enterprise. Shareholders demand that their investments in PR provide acceptable, or even outstanding, return on investments. PRM systems deliver reduced financial risks through improvements in control and use of the PR.

Documented processes increase efficiency and effectiveness of PR through repeatable and standardized execution of PRM work. PRMS must execute routine work each day in the most efficient ways to provide value to the enterprise. History is replete with failures of enterprises when key asset management processes are performed haphazardly or neglected over time. Documented processes provide necessary safeguards against lapsing performance in PRMS.

Records of PR are necessary for a variety of reasons. An example of a key need for records supporting maintenance and or operations are the records that contain data that is needed for understanding failure modes. Such records are critical to implement preventative maintenance to prevent failures or to effect repairs when items fail. Other key reasons for records include regulatory requirements for some types of PR that are reportable for environmental or other safety reasons. A critical safety requirement is documentation of things like brake inspections on motor equipment engaged in commerce regulated by governments. If brake inspections are not documented and an asset is involved in an accident the liability assignments back to the owner could be severe compared to an asset that had well documented brake inspections. These types of records needs are present throughout many types of PR used in the performance of work across the enterprise. As government regulations continue to increase these needs become more pressing and costly, efficient and effective PRMS provide value through providing this kind of information more effectively than other methods.

Audit trails of transactions have been a financial necessity for many publicly owned and government organizations for many years to meet safety, accounting, environmental, and other rules. Transaction audit trails document the history of assets from production through disposal. The requirement for tracking of vehicles by state and national governments is an excellent illustration of a transaction audit trail. The revenues created for governments through vehicle registration taxes are such that laws require that owners of vehicle PR register upon acquisition. After that initial registration using the unique identifier (the vehicle identification number), the owner must report transactions such as changes of ownership as long as the vehicle is used. This is one easy-to-understand transaction audit trail, and there are myriad of other types of PR that need the same type of audit trail. The reasons for the transaction audit trail vary, but the principle is the same as the vehicle illustration.

Services provided by the PRM system or functions vary widely as there are many potential services, and the need for PRMS to deliver the services is driven primarily by the needs of the organization.

Several key services that can be delivered by asset management systems and functions/organizations are:

- Analysis of asset data to produce customized information
- Notification of asset tasks due
- Review of asset or item usage/demand data
- Development of tables of asset authorizations for organizations
- Disposal services for other organizations within the entity

Procedures are more important in PRM systems than some other functional areas because the success of efficient life cycle asset management hinges on standardized repeatable processes working across the breadth of the enterprise. There must be a policy level, an enterprise-wide process level, and a practitioner level of procedures well documented and updated periodically.

The policy level should clearly state the executive level expectations regarding PRM. Key elements of the policy should address the authority for determining asset requirements and expectations regarding life cycle management. Executives at the highest level must establish the policy regarding prioritization of use of PR and describe the expectation that all personnel properly use PR to avoid mis-use and the increased costs associated with unavailability for operations.

The enterprise-wide process level of procedures provides for efficient and effective execution of PRM. This level of procedures stipulates, when necessary, standardization for decision making and execution of key controls. This level of documentation can be simple, but must be rigorous to avoid both less-than-acceptable availability of PR when needed and minimize loss of value due to neglect or inappropriate disposal.

CHAPTER 4 – HIGHLIGHTS

- **Accounting**

- **Operations**

- **Supply Chain Management**

The PRM system could be operated as a stand alone function, but this would not be very efficient or effective. Stand alone functions have been done, but they have proven to be costly and did not provide adequate stakeholder value. As much, or more, than other disciplines, PRM must integrate with other key functions. This is true more today than in the past because improvements in automated systems offer opportunities for use of the data from other functions to achieve PRM objectives. Key integration disciplines are: Supply Chain Management, Accounting, Operations, Maintenance, Physical Security, and Facility Management. All of these functions are both suppliers of information to and customers of the products and services of the PRM system.

Supply Chain Management

Acquisition processes provide critical information for the identification elements of the PRM systems. Procurement records and data are often sufficient for the identification and initial entry into the tracking of PR processes. Through integration with this discipline, cost effective PRM can begin at the point of requirement identification and more efficiently continue into the life cycle control of an asset.

Integration with the supply chain sourcing processes provides the opportunity to be sure that PR that currently exist are not duplicated unnecessarily. When PRM is properly integrated with the sourcing process, existing asset information is made available to organizations that have a need for an asset. In leading edge processes, asset information available to requestors would include capacity that is available for the requestor. For example, if a truck is needed by the production organization and the shipping organization has several trucks that are available twenty-five percent of the time for other departments to use, an arrangement could be made for production to borrow the trucks necessary for their needs and save the cost of buying a new asset.

Integration with the physical distribution functions of supply chain management is a critical area of PRM. Physical distribution functions include transportation and warehousing. These elements of supply chain management provide important services and products that are critical to managing physical resources.

The transportation world for PRMS usually begins with the completion of the acquisition phase. Once an item is on the way information about the item can be vital to several facets of PRM. For example, when an apparel item completes manufacturing and is shipped across the world on a ship the journey can be long with several stops along the way. This same item will likely be transported by truck, ship, and rail before reaching the final sales destination. Along the way it may be in storage for some periods of time at ports or distribution centers. Transportation systems can provide information regarding the location and expected delivery date in real time. This information can be vital to PRM as decisions regarding several facets such as inventory management, stock control, and storage will be affected by transportation information.

The traffic management elements of the transportation process deal with how items are transported. Traffic management systems determine modes, routes, carriers, and often provide in-transit information to the PRMS. Integration with the transportation and traffic management systems is integral for both supply chain management and PRM. When these systems are singing along with each other (integrated) significant efficiencies are achieved, when these systems are not integrated costs are usually higher. These supply chain costs can be discriminators between entities that affect the overarching cost of PRMS.

Warehousing activities store raw materials, supplies, and finished goods. The physical distribution actions of receipt, storage and issue of items can be expensive. Entities that need warehousing either use services provided by others, usually now called third party logistics (3PL) or they own and operate their own warehousing functions. Whether acquiring these services or operating their own the PRMS interface is primarily information. Warehousing functions must provide information about the types and volumes of items in storage. This information is critical to minimizing the cost of PR. If too much or too little is in storage there are impacts to the PRMS and to the mission of the entity.

Accounting

The accounting function often gathers and uses key data that can either be obtained from the PRM system or the accounting data can be used as part of the PRM system. In many companies, and especially when managing client owned, for example government owned PR, it is critical that the accounting records and PRM records be integrated. Integration of data eliminates duplication and provides for more accurate reporting of both accounting information and PR information.

Accounting records of PR are often viewed as the same as PRM records, but they are not the same. Accounting is concerned with the current cost and current value of PR. The current cost and value are not the same as original cost, replacement value, productivity, availability, and reliability of PR. As a result, reports of PR from accounting that are used by other organizations often fall short of their needs. In addition, accounting is not concerned with life cycle tracking of PR.

PRM should lead accounting and provide necessary data for creation of accounting records and then provide updates through the life cycle process to aid accounting in completing their important financial work. PRM functions that lead accounting will increase their value to the enterprise and improve stakeholder value.

Operations

The various facets of operations, including functions such as sales, facility management, and production, are key customers of the PRM systems. Integration with these functions is a critical aspect of effective PRM. These functions need the information provided by PRM. Sales needs to know inventory levels, facility management needs to know information about buildings and grounds, and operations needs to know how many PR, and their location, condition, and often their availability for use.

Operations' also provides critical data used by the PRM system to produce the information necessary to provide to customers. Operations' provides data in a variety of ways regarding asset location, condition, and availability that is converted to information needed to perform the work of the organization or company.

Business operations are those ongoing recurring activities involved in the running of a business for the purpose of producing value for the stakeholders. The outcome of business operations is the receipt of value from PR owned by a business. In this sense, PR can be either physical or intangible. An example of value derived from a physical asset like a building is rent. An example of value derived from an intangible asset like an idea is a royalty. Business operations encompass three fundamental management imperatives that collectively aim to maximize value from business

PR: generate recurring income, increase the value of the business PR, and secure the income and value of the business.

These imperatives are mutually dependent. The more recurring income an asset generates, the more valuable it becomes. For example, the products that sell at the highest volumes and prices are usually considered to be the most valuable products in a business's product portfolio. The more valuable a product becomes the more recurring income it generates. For example, a luxury car can be leased out at a higher rate than a normal car. The intrinsic value and income-generating potential of an asset is not realized without a way to secure it. For example, petroleum deposits are worthless unless processes and equipment are developed and employed to extract, refine, and distribute it profitably.

The business model of an entity describes the means by which the three management imperatives are achieved. In this sense, business operations is the execution of the business model. PRM is an essential part of an organization's business model.

Facility Management

Real Property, especially buildings and other structures are usually very expensive PR. The owners of commercial buildings need specialized functions and trained personnel to manage these PR. Facility Management is a discipline that is dedicated to operations of real property PR. Facility managers ensure that building

31

operations including power such as electrical substations and switchgear, emergency power systems, heating ventilation and air conditioning, life safety systems (alarms and fire suppression), and other monitoring systems operate effectively and efficiently ,

Along with building services, dealing with office spaces can also fall under the responsibility of the facilities department. These responsibilities often include maintenance and repair, and physical security of real property assets. Facility management interface with PRMS requires integration of information using products from inventory management and other services of PRMS.

Maintenance & Repair

The PRMS relationship with maintenance and repair is very important over the life of a physical asset, as products and services of PRMS are derived from data provided by maintenance activities and maintenance and activities in turn need information from PRMS. Different maintenance and repair activities have varied needs that drive the relationship with PRMS.

Maintenance is performing preventative actions on PR to prevent breakdowns or failures. Repairs are often considered part of maintenance, but are really not, as repair actions are taken to fix PR, usually equipment, when such PR become out of order or broken. Maintenance preventative work includes performing the routine actions such as oil changes, which keep engines in PR in working order and prevent operating trouble or failures. Reliability centered maintenance (RCM) for PR is accomplished through the use of predictive techniques in addition to traditional preventive measures. RCM techniques can result in a lower net present cost for entities to achieve a given level of performance for PR when acceptable risks are understood and managed. To evaluate physical asset condition, predictive maintenance techniques use nondestructive testing including on line and other specific tests.

Preventive maintenance is the physical performance of periodic servicing of PR. Preventative maintenance keeps certain PR, including facilities, in satisfactory operating condition. Preventative maintenance provides systematic inspection, detection, of incipient failures before they occur and potentially result in major defects.

The maintenance function uses several methods for determining what predictive maintenance or other failure management policies should be applied. Common methods are: original equipment manufacturer recommendations, requirements of safety or other codes and legislation, and engineering analysis completed to identify what should be done and when. Implementation of the most applicable and effective failure management policies are important PRM issues.

A primary goal of maintenance is to avoid or mitigate the consequences of either planned or unplanned asset failure to operate. In the course of a physical asset life cycle there are bound to be failures that require repair; this does not necessarily mean that the maintenance activities were at fault for this condition. When PR fail to operate repair actions are necessary. Repair operations can entail internal or external labor and usually require non-labor or other PR to fix the problem that has been encountered.

Physical Security

Physical security for PR describes measures that prevent or deter, either separately or in some combination, unauthorized individuals from accessing PR. Of course in our current technological age, many PR have information that is also very valuable embedded. So physical security coverage includes facilities, equipment, other physical asset categories, and information stored on physical media. Asset physical security techniques can be as simple as a locked door or as elaborate as multiple layers of armed personnel. For physical resource management, the field of security engineering has identified several key elements to physical security: These key elements are, explosion protection, obstacles, alarms, security lighting, or electronic monitoring, and personnel response. When a physical resource security system is well designed these features complement each other and four key aspects of physical security. These four key aspects of physical security are environmental design, physical controls, intrusion detection, and video monitoring.

Interrelated Disciplines

People are involved in all aspects of physical resource security systems. Many security personnel are guards that have a primary or support role in most aspects of security. People also administer electronic access controls and respond to alarms. Physical resource users often have a role also by questioning and reporting suspicious people. Today in many places photo ID badges are used and are frequently coupled to the electronic access control system. Visitors are often required to wear a visitor badge.

PRM integration with these six functions is critical because when there is no properly functioning PRM system all of these functions are likely to create duplicative processes to get the products and services they need to perform their missions. Many organizations have found this when they implement six sigma or other process improvement programs. When process flow maps are produced it is often noted that people in different departments are doing the same thing. When these processes are analyzed it is discovered that a central function could provide the same products and services at a lower cost. This is not a centralization versus decentralization issue; it is a pure duplication issue. When evaluating centralized versus decentralized functions it is recognized that duplication would be minimized in either case by good organization structure. In the case of a failure to have an effective PRM system, the issue is just waste due to ineffective duplicative systems performed across the enterprise.

CHAPTER 5 – HIGHLIGHTS

- **Acquisition**

- **Use**

- **Disposal**

The processes of PRM provide an organization with life cycle control of PR. Life cycle control provides for appropriate identification of needs which ensures optimal expenditures for material, utilization controls providing for maximum use of PR, and finally disposition controls which ensure optimal return on investment. The five life cycle functional areas of PRM are:

1) Requirement Identification,

2) Acquisition,

3) Asset Identification,

4) Use-operation and,

5) Disposal.

Definitions of these life cycle phases are described below.

Requirement Identification

The more asset intensive the organization the more business performance is affected by the availability and deployment of PR. In some entities even a few minutes or hours without necessary equipment can have a significant impact on operations and correlated financial results. Asset management is a critical element of the supply chain and good asset managers consistently deal with tough asset problems with their equipment and other items. But in many cases managers are spending important chunks of time reacting to emergencies and not planning ahead about how they will optimize their PR to achieve the best business performance.

In the requirements identification phase, planning ahead entails creating a PRMS strategy for each asset classification. The strategies must meet the competing demands of deployment, maintenance, financing, and performance to achieve the organization's operational goals. When the strategies are developed a key element is the early identification of requirements for PR. Once requirements are identified the decision to make or buy items is a critical early activity. Organizations that have production capacity may decide to make PR, and then the PRMS activities are part of the production process. When organizations determine that buying is the correct choice, the acquisition process kicks off and is extremely important to the PRMS.

The asset class strategy is created in the requirements identification life cycle phase and is then executed across the life cycle of the PR. The execution of the strategy is accomplished as part of the inventory management process discussed in chapter seven.

Acquisition

The acquisition process provides for the procurement of goods and/or services at the best possible cost in right quantity and quality, at the right time and place, and from the best source. Efficient and effective execution of acquisition processes provide

PR for the direct benefit or use of corporations, or individuals, generally via a contract. Simple procurement may involve nothing more than repeat purchasing. Complex procurement could involve finding sources for hard to get commodities and developing specialized contracts for procuring specially designed items.

Asset Identification

The process of asset identification sounds simple. And this process is not simply about applying a tag ("tagging") to items so that they can be identified. This process has proven to be the most critical aspect of PRM because if an item cannot be identified as requiring life cycle control it will not be managed. The failure to properly develop and implement this process has been the root cause of the failure of many PRM systems.

The modern acquisition world allows many people in an enterprise to purchase PR. The PRM system must know what methods an entity uses and ensure that necessary information is obtained to identify how PR should be managed. The current deployment of acquisition functions, aided by automated systems, includes simple acquisition methods such as credit cards for small items and complicated contracts for large capital equipment and real estate. The ability of PRM to corral the necessary information is simple and more efficient than ever before when automated techniques are employed.

PRM systems must employ data mining techniques to ensure the identification of PR to track. It has always been relatively easy to identify the categories of PR to track, such as: real estate, buildings, capital equipment, and stock material inventory. It has been a challenge to ensure that information about the acquisition of these items was obtained and used for tracking and controlling these items. Now through use of data mining, PR professionals can identify PR when they are ordered by getting data from the acquisition systems.

When automated data mining techniques can't be used it is usually because the systems won't perform or there is some kind of organizational problem. If automated systems can't be used then the old fashioned work-around processes are used to identify PR. These old fashioned processes include obtaining copies of acquisition or receiving documents, or establishing communication methods between organizations. These processes are slower, possibly less accurate, but can work if other methods are not feasible.

In addition, asset identification is the process most effectively used to ensure that the minimum numbers of PR are acquired to meet the needs of the organization. If this control process is not applied in some fashion it is likely that duplicative and costly PR will be acquired by the organization. This control process can be implemented in many ways, but all share a common theme of ensuring that available PR are completely used before acquisition of new PR. This is a critical element of cost control that will not be achieved without necessary information being made available for acquisition decision makers.

There are many acceptable methods of providing information to acquisition decision makers about available PR, but the organization must develop and enforce effective control methods to ensure that available PR are considered before acquisition of additional PR.

Asset Utilization

The effective use of PR to achieve the missions of the organization is key to sustaining the viability of the organization. The PRM processes for asset utilization encompass all types of PR from rubber bands to buildings. There are five primary categories of PR, with variations of these categories and variations of what is in the categories, but these five categories are generally accepted.

These key categories are:

1) Real Property,

2) Equipment,

3) Raw material,

4) Supplies, and

5) Finished goods.

The utilization processes are unique for each of the categories.

Real Property Physical Resources

Real property PR are usually the most costly and valuable asset that most entities have. Real property PR includes land, buildings, and other structures. These PR, whether leased or owned, require rigorous utilization controls. If an entity has either too many or not enough of these valuable PR it would usually mean the end of the entity. The logic of proportionality works for real PR as for the other key asset categories. For example, even in the case of a home based small business the real PR used, the owner's home, must be adequate for the needs or the small business will not survive. And for the largest entities having real PR that is not needed, or not having the needed PR, would be a resource drain that could impact the viability of the entity.

Equipment

Equipment is usually the next most expensive category of PR, but not always. Sometimes the equipment used for manufacturing or research could be more costly than the real PR it is on or in. Whether or not equipment is number one or number two in value the application of effective PRM is a winner for the owning entity. Installed equipment that doesn't move is a fairly simple utilization controlled item, but cannot be ignored. The availability of installed equipment, and the utilization rates, must be monitored and tracked to be sure of appropriate availability for production and financial considerations. For entities that use equipment for conducting their business an effective and efficient PRM system is a competitive advantage that could easily make or break them.

Raw Materials

Raw materials are needed for production of goods for sale, usually the primary processes of production businesses. PRM processes ensure that the appropriate techniques are used to determine requirements and then control the raw materials inventory levels. Over investment is a problem that can be avoided through asset utilization controls that identify, predict, and establish inventory levels that support production, but don't cost more than necessary. The organization's production management processes must include techniques for forecasting, sourcing, and acquiring raw materials that are synched up with authorized production schedules.

The PRM system must have administrative controls in place that provide cognizant senior management with assurances that independent reviews of inventory levels occur at a frequency that limits the risks of significant amounts of excess raw materials. The controls can usually be implemented by using data from acquisition plans, production plans and schedules, and accounting data on costs of raw material.

Supplies

The supply category includes items that are consumed in use, therefore they are not equipment. Supplies include items that are purchased and used directly and those that are stocked and then used. A high cost savings potential for supplies PRMS revolves around spare parts, while consumed in use, the resource investment in spare parts can be high. As with the other elements of PRM the supply category can range in the level of investment based on the type of activities of the entity. Organizations that have high volumes of supplies needs are most impacted by PRMS for this classification of items.

Finished Goods

Manufacturers produce items for sale. These items comprise finished goods inventory. These PR are extremely critical in the success of a manufacturing company and their ability to effectively manage this element of their PR is of vital importance to their viability.

Overall the PRM elements of work associated with managing supplies and finished goods is generally characterized as inventory or stock control. There are several important parts of inventory control that must work together in the PRM system to ensure that supplies and finished goods are properly controlled to meet operations needs and the needs of customers.

Disposal

PR have an end of useful life. Most, by volume of items, are consumed in use; these are often called consumables. These PR are either installed in another piece of equipment or a building or they are actually used up in use. An example of the former is a valve that is installed in an engine. The valve was likely tracked from need through receipt and storage and the end of the valves life as a separate item occurs at installation in the engine. Other items, such as small tools or other items used in production are either completely used up, e.g. a pencil. These items are just thrown into the trash when used up. But the most valuable PR are generally not consumed in use and when they are no longer required a disposal process that provides for some kind of return on the original investment provides value to the company.

PR disposal processes usually include reuse within the company or the broader corporation. Reuse is important if the asset is in good condition and another part of the organization needs the item; this extends the useful life and likely creates a cost savings as the organization in need will not need to acquire an item. If there is no need within the organization then donations or sales of PR are useful processes to provide either cash value – or for donations, goodwill value – as returns on the investment.

The disposal process has two branches: items that are used up or that become contaminated with hazardous materials are considered waste, and items that have use left, even as scrap, are considered reusable. Making an initial decision about waste or reuse for items when they are no longer needed determines which branch, waste or reusable, the item follows for disposal. The initial decision should take into account the costs of each branch. For example, an ink pen may be used up, yet is likely reusable, but the cost of reuse outweighs the benefit, therefore the ink pen would be thrown away as waste.

Waste Disposal of Physical Resources

Disposal of items as waste is as simple as throwing away a used pencil or as complicated as disposing of items that are contaminated with hazardous materials. Between these two extremes there are many variations. The simpler methods of throwing things away in the trash for disposal in municipal dumps are very economical; the primary costs are containers and labor to move to designated pickup areas and then the periodic costs for payment to the municipality or private trash company. The more complicated disposal of hazardous and/or large items cost much more to comply with the myriad environmental requirements. The costs to dispose of these types of items is often very high and should be factored into the life cycle strategies for such items.

Reuse Disposal of Physical Resources

Disposal of items that have value above the costs to execute the disposal actions are considered an element, and sometimes a very important element, of the life cycle costs of such items. Many PR that are reusable can generate income for the owner, and sometimes can be reused with a lower cost than disposal as waste providing value through cost avoidance.

The fundamental processes for disposal are deceptively simple. The steps are:

- Ensure that the item is not needed elsewhere in the entity, for those items that are worth keeping, usually meaning they are in good working order and worth the cost of handling to move to another location.

- Determine if the item is worth selling as one item or if it should part of aggregation of items, usually called a "lot".

- Sell the item and use the revenue to first offset the costs of disposal and the remainder for whatever purpose the entity desires.

As noted this is deceptively simple and it is something that is often outsourced; there are many companies that will sell your items and return much of the sales revenue. Often the sales return will exceed 90% of the sales price with the supplier for disposal keeping less than 10%. This is one of the cases where volume discounts are normal; the more items that are given to the disposal company the less they charge for selling the items.

CHAPTER 6 - HIGHLIGHTS

- **Description**

- **Levels**

- **Administrative**

PRM procedures should have different levels that deal with the overall entity and PRM internal operations. PRM procedures document the administrative controls for the organization's PR as well as describing processes to achieve standardized and repeatable operations. Execution of the processes to achieve desired outcomes is a key contribution toward operational excellence for the overall organization.

The discussion of procedures is of course intended only for entities that need procedures. A very small enterprise, or an enterprise that has few PR, probably does not need a lot of documentation on how PR are managed.

System Description

The enterprise should have a summary document that describes the PRM system. The system description should describe the scope of the function and the roles and responsibilities of the various organizational elements that are part of the system. Such a document has not been a staple of other management systems, and entities that allocate the resources to this endeavor in the 21st century will be leaders in managing their PR to deliver improved value to their stakeholders. This document is vital to making sure that the function meets its mission requirements. In the past, this documentation of management systems hasn't been considered very important, but in today's fast paced world filled with constant change, the work required to write this document will achieve a 100% return on investment.

Enterprise Level Procedures

Enterprise level procedures should set the rules for processes that must be uniform across the entity. Normally such procedures would cover controls about acquisition, receipt, usage, and disposal. Often an approach using manuals or guides is very efficient to ensure that standardized and repeatable processes are performed across the enterprise.

Operations Level Procedures

Operations level procedures will define the rules for processes performed by personnel, including PRM practitioners in their day-to-day work. This set of procedures is critical to producing the services and products of PRM. Some organizations (not usually very successful over the long term) believe that such procedures are not necessary. In the PRM function these procedures are mandatory and would include coverage of the entire life cycle of PR.

A simple example of why written operations level procedures are necessary can be seen in a problem related to the seemingly simple function of asset identification. In some organizations, let's say Company A, a desktop computer might be considered an asset that requires tracking if a critical product production was based on the availability of desk top computers. In other organizations, say Company B, tracking desktop computers might not be important as they are considered a secondary tool and are not critical in production. If the procedures don't exist and an experienced person is hired from Company B to Company A, one of two things would have to occur to avoid an impact to production. Someone would need to train the person, a costly proposition for each change in personnel, or a procedure would need to exist.

Administrative Controls

Many functions have the need for administrative controls. In the PRM system administrative controls are the primary mechanisms that protect the investment in PR for most organizations. Other controls including physical security, transactional controls, and access limitations are discussed in the life cycle control section.

Many disciplines have need of procedures to achieve standardized repeatable operations. PRM is no different. The procedures must be specifically written for the organization as many PRM activities must be integrated with other operations that usually are not standard. The procedures should ensure conformance with accepted industry standards. The ASTM provides the commercial standards and the government standards are provided in various requirements documents. The ISO has some standards regarding management of PR, especially focused on controlling and accounting for PR of clients controlled by an organization.

CHAPTER 7 – HIGHLIGHTS

- **Strategy**

- **Life Cycle Control**

- **Functions**

The processes of PRM provide an organization with life cycle control of PR. Life cycle control provides for appropriate identification of need which ensures optimal expenditures for material, utilization controls which provide for maximum use of PR, and finally disposition controls which ensure optimal return on investment. This chapter describes the implementation and operation of processes to implement the five life cycle functional areas of PRM. The five life cycle functional areas are described in chapter five. These functional areas are: 1) Requirement Identification, 2) Acquisition, 3) Asset Identification, 4) Use-operation and 5) Disposal.

Requirement Identification Processes

In the requirement identification process, the primary activity is the creation of a PRMS strategy for each asset classification. The strategies must meet the competing demands of deployment, maintenance, financing, and performance to achieve the organization operational goals. When the strategies are developed a key element is the early identification of requirements for PR. Once requirements are identified the decision to make or buy items is a critical early activity. Organizations that have production capacity may decide to make PR, and then the PRMS activities are part of the production process. When organizations determine that buying is the correct choice the acquisition process kicks off and is extremely important to the PRMS.

PRM Strategy Development

PRM strategies involve determining the approaches for how PR will be acquired, utilized and disposed. Each asset class, or costly item (for example buildings or production lines that cost millions of dollars) demands the planning work necessary to develop the strategies for best PRM. Completing this planning activity before acquisition is ideal, but even later is better than never for items that have long life or that are acquired repetitively.

PRM strategies are developed by executing basic planning methods that are customized for asset management. Planning in PRM is both the organizational process of creating and maintaining a plan, and the psychological process of thinking about the activities required to create a desired goal. The planning process is essential to the creation and refinement of a plan, or integration of it with other plans; that is, it combines forecasting of developments with the preparation of ways to react to expected situations.

The PRM strategic plan for each asset class should be a realistic view of the forecasted expectations. Depending upon the volume in terms of cost or value of PR the PRM strategy can be long range, intermediate range or short range. This early decision creates the framework within which the PRM strategy must operate. Each PRM strategy should be documented in a plan; the plan then becomes a very important document and key to executing efficient and effective PRM lifecycle activities. Preparation of a comprehensive plan will not guarantee success, but lack of a sound plan will almost certainly ensure failure.

Just as no two organizations are alike, PRM strategies can also be different even within an organization that has diverse asset operations. It is therefore important to prepare a plan keeping in view the necessities of the asset operations. The PRM asset class plan serves the three critical functions.

These functions are:

- Clarifies and focuses PRM actions on organizational successes.

- Provides a considered and logical framework within which PRM activities are conducted.

- Delivers a benchmark against which actual performance can be measured and reviewed.

A plan can play a vital role in helping to avoid mistakes or recognize hidden opportunities. Preparing a satisfactory PRM strategies plan for asset classes is essential to successful PRM within an enterprise. The planning process enables PRM management to understand more clearly what they want to achieve, and how and when they can do it.

A well-prepared PRM strategic plan demonstrates that the managers know the business and that they have thought through its development in terms of mission support, products, finances, and most importantly, contributions to the entity's overall success.

Acquisition

The acquisition process provides for the procurement of goods and/or services at the best possible cost in right quantity and quality, at the right time and place, from the best source for the direct benefit or use of corporations, or individuals, generally via a contract. Simple procurement may involve nothing more than repeat purchasing. Complex procurement could involve finding sources for hard to get commodities and developing specialized contracts for procuring specially designed items.

Most purchasing decisions include factors such as delivery and handling, marginal benefit, and price fluctuations. Procurement generally involves making buying decisions considering competing needs and goals regarding timing and prices. Processes are implemented in procurement systems to balance risk in cost and schedule to meet organizational needs.

Procurement systems

Procurement systems are needed so that entities get the best value for their acquisition expenditures; it costs money to buy things and services, and procurement systems are how such costs are controlled. Our focus is of course the purchasing of PR. The basics of purchasing are relatively simple, almost everyone is a consumer and we know how to buy what we need. When organizations need to buy things it can be as simple as what we do at home. In the case of large companies or institutions, however, systems are needed to ensure the best bang for the buck. In order to achieve greater economies of scale an organization's procurement functions may be joined with other organizations into shared services. This method combines several small procurement agents into one centralized procurement system.

Procurement may also involve bidding processes. When a company needs to purchase a product, and the cost for that product/service is over the threshold that has been established (e.g. "any product/service desired that is over $1,000 requires a bidding process"), the contract is opened to the competitive bidding process. The process may have ten submitters that state the cost of the product/service they are willing to provide. Then, the purchasing agent will usually select the best value bid. Best value is determined by a set of conditions including price, quality, responsiveness, and other factors.

Procurement Process Steps

There are generally five steps in the routine acquisition process for buying of PR. These five steps are:

- Sourcing: If the potential customer does not already have an established relationship with sales/ marketing functions of suppliers of needed PR, it is necessary to search for suppliers who can satisfy the requirements.

- Supplier Contact: When one or more suitable suppliers for the PR have been identified contact is made. Common actions for this contact are: Requests for Quotation (RFQ), Requests for Proposals (RFP), Requests for Information (RFI) may be published to obtain information from suppliers.

- Due Diligence: A background review may need to be conducted to be sure the supplier has a good history and sound financial foundations. The purchasing organization obtains references and examines supplier history for providing follow-up services such as installation, maintenance, and warranty fulfillment. Samples of the PR being considered may be examined, or tests conducted. .

- Contract Development: Negotiations are conducted, and price, availability, and other specifics for the buy are established. Delivery schedules are negotiated, and a contract to acquire the asset is completed.

- Order Fulfillment: Supplier preparation, shipment, delivery, and payment for the asset are completed, based on contract terms. Installation and training may also be included.

Asset Identification

If an organization does not have a method to identify PR early in their life cycle it is not likely that the PR will be properly managed and fully utilized. When PR are poorly managed the costs to maintain and control them are almost certainly going to be higher than well managed PR. Value added asset management provides for early identification of PR and puts them into control even before physical receipt.

Early identification and introduction of control processes results in providing information to acquisition decision makers about available PR. This information ensures that items that are not truly needed are not acquired. In addition to providing the information, the organization must develop and enforce effective control methods to ensure that available PR are considered before acquisition of additional PR.

Asset Identification Process

As noted in the overview section on asset identification, the process of asset identification sounds simple. And this process is not simply about applying a tag ("tagging") to items so that they can be identified. This process has proven to be the most critical aspect of PRM because if an item cannot be identified as requiring life cycle control it will not be managed. The failure to properly develop and implement this process has been the root cause of the failure of many PRM systems.

There are many acceptable methods of providing information to acquisition decision makers about available PR, but the organization must develop and enforce effective control methods to ensure that available PR are considered before acquisition of additional PR. Additional details for how to identify PR are included in the inventory management section below.

Asset Utilization

The effective use of PR to achieve the mission of the organization is critical to sustaining the viability of the organization. Asset utilization in the broadest sense, which looks at how well PR are used to make a profit or meet the mission of the organization, measures an entity's ability to make best use of its resources and by inference, the quality of its management.

Good financial figures may disguise inefficiency up to a point, but when the relationship between investment in PR is analyzed closely, it often reveals how well or badly an organization is really managed. Broadly stated, for organizations that have intensive levels of PR their ability to operate is based on how well they manage PR or that is, perform operations.

The key metric for asset utilization comes from the balance sheet or profit and loss statements, so results can be compared with those of competitors, and with the industry as a whole. The real value in asset utilization metrics is in comparing an organization's performance to the appropriate industry data. For example, if the industry average is 7 days for inventory turnover, then a company achieving 5 days is better than average. As well as using the measure of asset utilization to assess performance, employers often reward their managers on the strength of the results.

Asset utilization is expressed in a series of ratios (also known as activity ratios), each of which examines a different aspect of the asset utilization relationship. The combination of ratios used may vary, depending on the context, but commonly include those that also stand alone like inventory turn over. Typically, a series of asset utilization ratios will include:

Income / Real PR: describes how effectively management utilizes real PR to create value to the entity. A higher result is generally better.

Depreciation / PR: expresses an assessment of how rapidly PR deteriorate (not in the financial/tax perspective) in utility for the mission, expressed as a percentage. A lower percentage is usually preferred.

Real PR / Total PR: measures the proportion of an organization's PR tied up in longer-term resources like plant, equipment and land.

Asset Depreciation / Income: indicates the percentage of income needed to cover wear and tear or depreciation of PR. A lower number is desirable.

Revenue / PR: shows how effectively PR are used to create income. A higher result is better.

Inventory Turnover: this measures the cost of goods sold (COGS) against inventory. The result is expressed in turnover, either items or dollars, and a higher number is better.

For organizations that have maintenance, repair, and operations support inventories (often service organizations, or others that aren't producing inventory for sale), inventory turnover is expressed in terms of number of items issued compared with total items. In this case the formula is:

Number of items/items issued.

If items are 10,000 and items issued in the period are 1,000 then:

$$10,000/1,000 = 10$$

As with all such calculations, asset utilization ratios become more meaningful over a period of time to create a trend, rather than using a single snapshot in time for analysis. Advances in automation have reduced the time and effort needed to calculate all these ratios and PR relationships. Regular asset utilization analysis using the appropriate ratios for the operation of the entity will help to keep track of their performance.

Inventory Management

Developing and implementing the strategy for each asset class or item is how inventory management as a key element of PRM creates lasting value compared to past practices and the old view of inventory management as stock control. In the past, inventory management was relegated to what should properly be called stock control. Managing asset inventories is not about the stock kept by organizations, it is about delivering value to stake-holders through reduced life cycle costs of PR. Properly managing PR through application of inventory management techniques during the utilization life cycle phase is at the heart of an effective PRMS.

The primary objective of inventory management of PR is to ensure availability of necessary items at the minimum cost. This must be done through application of trade off analyses against competing objectives. There are three objectives to be balanced in inventory management decisions and resulting operations. The purpose of implementing techniques to properly balance these objectives is to optimize support to the business operation of the entity. When these objectives are properly balance the goal of delivering value to the organization through PRMS is substantially achieved. When the goal is achieved the organization will have a competitive advantage or distinctive in asset management.

The three objectives for inventory management operations to balance and deliver the goal of adding value through PRMS are:

- Asset Availability

- Asset Cost

- Operating Cost

The awesome challenge is to add value while not optimizing any one of these objectives at the expense of the others. This is not a case of pick two out of three, with the classic options of good, cheap, and fast. Each objective must be balanced and weighted based on mission needs. For example, buying enough items so that production can have 100% availability for an item that only needs 85% availability would result in increases in both asset and operating costs, making them too high. But, when 100% availability is necessary to meet production needs, the asset and operating costs would not be too high; they would, by definition, be necessary. To provide the optimum amount of PR at the optimum costs requires that inventory management operations implement the asset strategy developed in the requirements identification life cycle phase. Also, in the inventory management function is the key activity of asset identification, which is discussed in detail in this chapter. The asset strategy options and resultant inventory management processes for each class of PR creates a dynamic that will transform an entity's PRM system into a distinct competitive advantage.

Asset Identification

Every organization needs to know what they have. The first step in creating the knowledge of PR is identification. No matter the size of the enterprise, some method of asset identification is necessary. For small organizations a periodic look around the operation and documenting what PR are on hand is a great way to identify PR. For larger organizations things are likely more complicated, but the process is still best if it is simple.

The modern acquisition world allows many people in an enterprise to purchase PR. The PRM system must provide methods that an entity uses and ensure that necessary information is obtained to identify how PR should be managed. Although the modern deployment of acquisition functions, aided by automated systems, includes simple acquisition methods, such as credit cards for small items and complicated contracts for large capital equipment and real estate, the ability to corral the necessary information is simpler than ever.

PRM systems must employ data mining techniques to ensure the identification of PR to track. It has always been relatively easy to identify the categories of PR to track, such as: real estate, buildings, capital equipment, and stock material inventory. It has been a challenge to ensure that information about the acquisition of these items was obtained and used for tracking and controlling these items. Now, through use of data mining PR, professionals can identify PR when they are ordered by getting data from the acquisition systems.

Automated Asset Identification

When large volumes of PR are used by an entity, automated processes are almost always more efficient and effective yield lower costs than manual process. In the case of automated asset identification, data mining is the best practice. Data mining is the process of sorting through large amounts of data and picking out relevant information. It is normally used to help make asset management decisions based on the patterns and forecasts generated from the data collected. This automated technique is both an art and science for extracting useful information from large data sets or databases.

Data mining in relation to PRM is the statistical and logical analysis of large sets of transaction data, looking for patterns that can aid in identification of PR and decision making about these PR.

Traditionally, business analysts have performed the task of extracting useful information from recorded data, but the increasing volume of data in today's increasingly automated world requires more automated, computer-based approaches. As data sets have grown in size and complexity, there has been a shift away from direct hands-on data analysis toward indirect, automatic data analysis using more complex and sophisticated tools. Advancements in computer technology have aided data collection. Automation can also aid in analyzing the captured data so that it can be converted into information and knowledge to become useful.

Data mining techniques identify trends within data that go beyond the simple analysis processes of the past. Through the use of sophisticated algorithms, asset management practitioners that are not statisticians have the opportunity to identify key attributes of business processes and target opportunities to identify PR early in the life cycle. Although data mining is a relatively new term, the technology is not. For some time, organizations have used computer-based processes to sift through volumes of data, such as supermarket scanner data. This data has been used to produce many types of reports that have been used to improve productivity and especially to identify trends and develop actions to interdict the trends much sooner than in the past. Over time, continuous innovations in computer processing power, disk storage, and statistical software have dramatically increased the accuracy and usefulness of data analysis.

For asset identification, the term data mining is used in application for two separate processes of knowledge discovery and prediction. Knowledge discovery provides explicit information that has a readable form and can be understood by a user. Organizations are accumulating vast and growing amounts of data in different formats and different databases.

These data sets include: operational or transactional data such as, sales, cost, inventory, payroll, and accounting. Non-operational data, such as industry sales, forecast data, and macro-economic data. Application of the knowledge discovery data is used to make predictions about a data set that are very useful in pulling only the information needed by an analyst to identify PR early in acquisition processing.

Asset Identification Algorithms

There are various data mining algorithms which can be used to build the asset identification mining model, but choosing the right algorithm for the asset identification task is critical to success. Different algorithms can be used to do the same business tasks but each algorithm produces different results. A data mining application can adopt different algorithms for different functions.

Asset identification requires gathering data from large data sets, and different algorithms are used for asset identification when working with such data sets. For example, we can use segmentation algorithms for exploring data and association algorithms to identify multiple attributes about items. Armed with multiple attributes the PRM decisions about asset identification are made with less labor costs and more accuracy.

There are several types of data mining algorithms that are potentially useful for physical asset identification. These physical asset identification algorithms are:

- Regression – this algorithm type predicts one or more continuous variables, such as physical asset life of x or y based on other attributes in the dataset.

- Sequence analysis – this algorithm type summarizes frequent sequences in data, such as a process path flow for PR.

- Segmentation – this algorithm type divides data into groups, or clusters, for identification of PR that have similar properties.

- Classification – this algorithm type predicts one or more discrete variables, based on the other attributes in the dataset.

- Association – this algorithm type finds correlations between different attributes in a dataset. Using this algorithm to create association rules for types of physical assets within data for use in identification technical analysis.

Manual Methods of Asset Identification

When automated techniques can't be used it is usually because the systems won't perform or there is some kind of organizational problem. If automated systems can't be used, then the old fashioned manual methods are used to identify PR. These manual methods can be effectively used in any size organization, but they become very inefficient as the number of items acquired increases. The manual process generally entails some type of review of items acquired by a human. This process can be a complete review, or a review of only items that meet some type of criteria. Unless the organization is very small this approach will require coordination across multiple organizations.

Coordination with the purchasing or receiving organization is generally the key to manual processes for asset identification. In the best scenario the people responsible for asset identification receive a report of items acquired or received and then determine through analysis which items require additional PRM actions. When reports are not available, some other form of review of either acquisitions or receipts is needed. In one real world example, somewhat the worst case scenario, personnel responsible for asset identification would review requisitions in advance of acquisition. This is an old fashioned approach that gets the job done, but would likely delay acquisition processing. If automated reporting processes are not available, a better approach would be manual reviews of either purchase orders or receiving reports to identify PR requiring additional PRM actions.

Once the items are identified as requiring additional PRM attention specific actions can be determined and implemented to meet organizational PRMS requirements. Another element of asset identification is that this process can ensure that the minimum numbers of PR are acquired to meet the needs of the organization. If this control process is not applied in some fashion it is likely that duplicative and costly PR will be acquired by the organization. This control process can be implemented in many ways, but all share a common theme of ensuring that available PR are completely used before acquisition of new PR. This is a critical element of cost control that will not be achieved without necessary information being made available for acquisition decision makers.

There are many acceptable methods of providing information to acquisition decision makers about available PR, but the organization must develop and enforce effective asset identification processes and methods to ensure that available PR are considered before acquisition of additional PR to optimize investments in PR.

Inventory Management for Real PR

Real property PR is the usually the most costly and valuable asset class that most entities have. Real property PR include: land, buildings, and other structures. In the requirements identification phase an asset strategy for this class of items will be developed. At the point the asset strategy is created the work of inventory begins. The asset strategy for real PR will revolve around ensuring that these large investments are utilized to a high percentage of capacity.

The real PR asset strategy considerations matrix is shown in figure 7.1 on the next page.

Element	Description	Life Cycle Phase Impact	Inv Management Process Impact
Criticality	Determine how important this real PR asset is for the organization. Is this only manufacturing plant or is it 1 of 10?	2) AQ 4) UO 5) DP	Responsibility Assignment Utilization Rates Failure mode alerts
Life Span	Determine the expected life of the real PR asset. Often the useful life of this class of PR is measured in decades.	4) UO 5) DP	Maintenance Confirmation Disposal Plan
Replacement	Determine when the item is expected to require replacement. Not all real PR items are alike. A stand alone pump house will likely require replacement before the manufacturing plant that it supports.	1) RI 5) DP	Timely completion of RI Timely completion of disposal plan

Legend: 1) Requirements Identification (RI), 2) Acquisition (AQ), 3) Asset Identification (AI),

4) Use-operation (UO), and 5) Disposal (DP)

Figure 7.1 Real PR Strategy IM Considerations

Inventory management (IM) for real PR includes several important functions that when properly executed in the organization's PRM create value for the entity. These unique functions for real PR should be identified in the strategy plan. Once identified in the strategy plan, remember this is done in the requirements identification phase, which occurs before the real PR asset is made or bought, the successful reliable performance of these inventory management actions ensures that the asset achieves it's mission.

The first inventory management action for real PR is responsibility assignment. This action identifies which organization within the entity, and usually which person within the organization, has the responsibility for the real PR asset. In the case of buildings this is usually the facility manager. This is not a binary situation, many times if a building is dedicated to one operation, for example the presses of a newspaper, the publisher, or another senior manager might be designated with the responsibility for the asset. It is important to the entity to identify the individual responsible for real PR to be sure that routine and extraordinary things like maintenance and repairs are completed in a timely fashion. The IM function tracks the responsibility assignment changes throughout the life of the real PR asset.

Inventory management almost always includes development and monitoring of utilization rates. For real PR this typically entails asset utilization ratios. There are three key examples of utilization ratios that are particularly useful for real PR.

These three key examples of utilization ratios are:

- Income or Revenue / Real PR: shows how effectively PR is used to create income or revenue. A higher result is desired, a low number could be a problem indicator.

- PR/ Real PR: shows the proportion of an organization's PR tied up in longer-term resources.

- Real PR Depreciation / Sales: shows the percentage of sales needed to cover wear and tear or utilization of PR. A lower number is desirable.

Real PR inventory management must also include processes that provide management with failure mode alerts. Failure mode alerts are needed when inventory management processes analyze utilization ratios and determine that the PR are not performing within the acceptable range. The acceptable range will need to be determined in advance and adjusted regularly to be relevant to actual conditions. For example if PRM system managers have designated that the PR/Real PR ratio should be X or lower and IM monitoring and analysis detects that the PR/Real PR ratio is W that would indicate a failure mode alert is created. When the failure mode alert condition is created it is then necessary to communicate the condition to PRM system management.

Inventory management processes for PR must monitor maintenance and repair completion as these actions affect the current condition of the PR. This IM process essentially ensures that the entity's PR are maintained at the optimum condition to meet overall mission objectives. Facility managers or other functional organizations actually plan and execute the maintenance and repair work, but generally these functions are focused on individual or smaller groups of PR. PRMS and IM develop and execute processes to ensure that classes of PR retain value necessary to meet organizational tactical objectives and strategic goals. As with utilization ratios described above when IM monitoring and analysis detect that a failure mode within maintenance or repair has or will occur that negatively affects the condition of real PR an alert mechanism for PRMS management is necessary to ensure that the condition is communicated.

In the final life cycle phase of real PR, IM determines the disposal processes and initiates requirements identification for replacements of the PR. When the functional utility of an PR asset is reached, either through age or changes to the entity missions the PR must be disposed to provide the greatest return on the investment in the item. IM processes are implemented before the final disposal and then if the asset needs replacement the requirements identification life cycle phase for the replacement is started finishing life of the current asset.

Inventory Management for Equipment

The asset category of equipment can often be almost as big an investment as real PR, or in some cases even most expensive category of PR, especially when the organization does not need a large amount of real PR. Sometimes the equipment used for manufacturing or research could be more costly than the real PR it is on or in.

As with real PR, the asset strategy for the equipment class of PR the strategy for managing these items will be developed in the requirements identification phase. At the point the asset strategy is created the work of inventory management for equipment begins. The asset strategy for equipment will revolve around ensuring that the correct IM actions are taken for either large single equipment items, or groups of smaller items that collectively are a large investment. The IM activities for equipment items bring into play the three competing priorities of IM.

These three competing priorities for equipment are:

- Asset Availability - for equipment this generally means that the items such as vehicles, material handling equipment, or production equipment are at the right place at the right time to support operations.

- Asset Cost - equipment cost is one of the tougher variables to deal with, the issues range from initial cost & quality, to warranty considerations and trade offs for maintenance model decisions.

- Operating Cost - costs to operate equipment generally revolve around optimizing availability and maintenance and repair activities, but also have a high number of variables.

Inventory management aspects for equipment revolve around utilization to meet mission need. The investment in this category of PR generally means that utilization is important but the variability is whether utilization or availability is more vital to support the organization's mission.

The equipment category asset strategy considerations matrix is shown in figure 7.2 on the next page.

Element	Description	Life Cycle Phase Impact	Inv Management Process Impact
Criticality	Determine how important the equipment asset or set of PR is for the organization's mission. Often critical equipment can be duplicated or kept at a high rate of availability through use of reports for quick repairs. Is this only manufacturing line or is it 1 of 10?	1) RI 2) AQ 4) UO	Responsibility Assignment Utilization Rates Availability Rates
Life Span	Determine the expected life of the equipment items. The useful life for this class of PR is usually measured in years.	4) UO	Maintenance Confirmation Failure mode alerts
Replacement	Determine when the item is expected to require replacement. Equipment items have a fair amount of difference in lifespan.	5) DP	Timely completion of disposal plan

Legend: 1) Requirements Identification (RI), 2) Acquisition (AQ), 3) Asset Identification (AI), 4) Use-operation (UO), and 5) Disposal (DP)

Figure 7.2 Equipment PR Strategy IM Considerations

Inventory management (IM) for equipment PR comprises several important processes that must be smartly executed as part of the organization's PRM to create the best value for the entity. The unique equipment inventory management functions that will be executed provide a streamlined way for company executives to know if their investments in equipment have paid off and to ensure that use and operation of the equipment is focused and effective in supporting the mission.

Identification of the IM processes that must be implemented to achieve optimized utilization of equipment should usually be completed in the requirements identification phase when the asset class strategy is developed. The completion of IM processes is not as critical for equipment items as for real PR and in addition the variability of cost of equipment also allows for logical variability when IM process identification is necessary. For example, a multi-million dollar item of equipment for a hospital that is used to keep patients alive would dictate that IM processes be identified early, the driver for early identification would be based on availability needs and cost. Another example when a later IM process identification is appropriate would be several items of equipment for a hospital that have a similar combined multi-million dollar cost, but are used for more routine diagnostics and in addition have redundancy due to multiple items available at the same geographic area or location. The drivers for IM processes in this case would be utilization and cost over availability of each item.

The initial IM action for equipment, similar to real PR is responsibility assignment. This action identifies which organization within the entity, and usually which person within the organization, has the responsibility for the equipment item. A real difference in this aspect of inventory management is that keeping up to date information on the physical owner/user of an equipment item is more efficient and effective in today's "e-world" and reduces the need for some other types of tracking that were used in the old days.

A key distinction for equipment inventory management compared to real PR is that often equipment items are mobile. This mobility difference requires that tracking systems account for the changes in location, user, and other key characteristics. An important element of equipment inventory management is configuration changes and associated record updates. This must be done for both operations support, after all if an operation needs a piece of equipment it must know where to obtain it for use, and for physical accountability and financial accounting.

Inventory management processes for equipment must monitor maintenance and repair completion just as with real PR items, as these actions affect the current condition of the PR. This IM process essentially ensures that the entities equipment PR are maintained at the optimum condition to meet overall mission objectives. The equipment user organizations or in large enterprises the maintenance organization or other functional organizations actually plan and execute the maintenance and repair work, but generally these functions are focused on individual or smaller groups of PR vice the overall outlook of IM and PRMS.

As with real PR, one of the value added areas that IM processes create as part of PRMS is failure mode alerts. When asset use is meeting the tactical objectives and this is impacting strategic goals for equipment PR IM processes must produce alerts for management necessary to ensure that the condition is communicated in a timely fashion so that corrective actions can be implemented to correct the conditions. IM develop and execute processes to ensure that classes of PR retain value necessary to meet organizational tactical objectives and strategic goals.

In the final life cycle phase of equipment PR IM determines the disposal processes and initiates requirements identification for replacements of the PR. When the functional utility of equipment items ends, either through age or changes to the entity missions, asset disposal actions must be identified and executed to provide the greatest return on the investment in the item. IM processes are implemented before the final disposal and then if the asset needs replacement the requirements identification life cycle phase for the replacement is started finishing life of the current asset.

Inventory Management for Raw Materials

Raw materials are needed for production operations the PRMS value added for this classification of PR is centered on inventory management activities. IM processes ensure that appropriate levels of these PR are acquired and maintained to meet production needs at the optimum cost. In the case of raw materials for production IM activities may include a significant amount of information about items that are not physically present at the company's facilities.

IM for raw materials pulls information from planning and analysis is performed to anticipate needs. IM interfaces with the supply chain activities and may actually manage items from their off-site storage or aggregation points right into the production operation. Production may need regular deliveries via the supply chain in a just in time manner to preclude storage of these items. IM processes would use economic order models and other techniques to ensure that the correct amount of items were at the origin point, in transit, and at the production location at all times to meet needs. This type of inventory management is what provides true value to the enterprise for raw materials.

The value proposition for raw material IM processes center around the requirements identification and use life cycle phases. Utilization rates and other metrics are really production oriented for this class of PR and are much more focused than for real PR and equipment. Utilization is really based on production having the amount of raw material needed to perform operations. Entities that don't have production operations would not typically need raw materials and therefore some of the other PRMS life cycles such as asset identification and disposal are rarely a part of the IM processes for these PR.

The fact that the IM processes are tightly focused and don't need utilization rates and disposal plans and processes does not diminish the needs for excellent IM work. PRMS adaptability and scaling functions are part of the overall value that this discipline provides to organizations that have needs for only some of the aspects. PRMS strategies for the raw material asset class is the key to identification of necessary work and scaled implementation to ensure that the optimum costs for PRM are realized.

For organizations that have large scale production activities the IM processes, while not addressing the breadth of the life cycle, are intense and deep in analysis of needs. When the needs are properly identified and plans are developed and executed the IM monitoring and failure mode processes become most critical to daily operations. IM failure mode communications, trumpeting the information about missed shipment or transit delays, become vital to management activities. PRMS value in this instance is usually proven in a highly visible way each day.

Inventory Management for Supplies

Supplies are used by the vast majority of organizations. Even the smallest of entities usually use some type of supplies. The IM processes for supplies depend mightily on the volume of items and the type of use. For example, the large production operations need supplies for workers to use, for example coveralls and gloves, as well as nuts, bolts, petroleum, oils, and lubricants, and so on. Companies that provide after market services for the goods that they sell, even organizations that provide only services to others, have a vital need for supplies and materials for repair and operations. The IM processes for supplies also revolve around volume of need, geographic, and organizational considerations more than any other asset class.

IM processes for supply start with activities in requirement identification that are vital throughout the life cycle. In this phase IM processes are part of the earliest aspects of this work. In the RI phase IM must determine, often for large quantities of items, exactly what is needed, by whom, how often, and where. When these fairly complex objectives are met the supply item life cycle begins. For example, when a printer is designed the number (within defined parameters) of pages that can be printed with an ink cartridge is determined. When an entity buys a printer (or printers) it can calculate how many pages will be printed within a time range and then determine how many ink cartridges will be needed over any time period. If the entity has procured several hundred printers for operations across their North American operations then the complexity is increased, but the requirements can still be identified. In this case in RI the organization must determine the strategy for these items around how these will be procured as needed, stocked for use, or provided by another organization (as in the case of services that provide maintenance &

repair of printers they would then do this same exercise to support their customers). The IM processes then synthesize this data to determine supply needs for ink cartridges as part of the RI phase.

In the next life cycle phase, the acquisition phase, IM processes are used to determine acquisition rules and processes for supplies. Carrying on the example from above with ink cartridges for printers IM analysis is used to identify total needs within time periods. This total entity need can then be used to develop economic order quantities. Economic order quantities, for large volume items can be developed that so significantly impact the life cycle cost of a supply item that this process alone can justify an organizations PRMS. By determining the breakpoint for most economical ordering volume discounts for item pricing, shipping, storage and delivery can be achieved that could for significant volumes over time reduce the costs for a supply item very dramatically, freeing up resources for other beneficial uses.

For supplies, the asset identification life cycle phase IM processes generally apply to large volume organizations. In small volume enterprises this phase is not usually needed. IM processes for asset identification of supplies produce value by identification of supplies that are not being managed in an optimum fashion. This is accomplished through data mining of acquisitions from across the large complex entity. When supplies are found being acquired and managed in less than optimum ways IM processes can be developed for each line item. Implementation of new acquisition and use processes are then key IM value added propositions that increase utilization rates and reduce life cycle costs.

IM processes for supplies really pay off in the use life cycle phase. Again this generally applies only to high volume supply users. In addition the greatest use of IM processes in the supplies category is for spare parts. Organizations that need spare parts must make an investment in these PR to perform their primary mission. Spare parts can be a costly investment either because of the volume needed, the item cost, or the critical nature of their availability to the mission. A key element of the use life cycle is the decision regarding supply chain/logistics issues regarding self stocking or just in time delivery. When an organization needs supplies to perform it's primary mission, it really needs them on time every time. IM processes for use revolve around having functionality that can identify the parameters of items, usually through a catalog. In today's world this catalog will be automated, but the key parameters are the same.

IM must know about the supply items, locations, quantities, and storage/delivery methods. The catalog function is key to IM processes. Supply items are identified through asset identification techniques and then a catalog is started with basic information captured and then analysis is conducted to determine the key characteristics of an item of supply, these key data are captured in a catalog data base. From these key catalog/record data supply item inventory management processes must be implemented that acquire, stock, issue, and then replenish and start the cycle again in a precise manner with high rates of accuracy. These standardized repeatable IM processes are what keeps organizations that need supplies swimming, or if these don't work well, sinking. The value of PRMS is ratified every day for supply intensive entities.

The final life cycle phase for supplies is disposal. Ideally, this activity only consists of removal of the catalog or data base record. This ideal is only reached when the supply asset has been physically depleted. If this ideal condition is not reached, then the process includes physical removal and disposal of unused supply items from the physical stock or storage locations. Then the disposal action is biased to whatever the best return on investment for the remaining items. This is basically either return to the manufacturer, sale, or sending the items to the landfill, following all applicable environmental regulations of course. Generally when a supply item has reached end of life there is no need for replacement, and so there is no need to wrap back around to the RI life cycle phase.

Finished Goods Inventory Management

Entities that are manufacturers produce items to sell. These finished goods require inventory management processes that are much different than the other asset categories. For this class of PR the IM processes start with completion of production. Items have distribution channels that take them to the final sales point. Some items go to distributors for resale to other companies or consumers. Some organizations are both producers and distributors selling their own merchandise to other companies or consumers. In either case the IM processes are very similar.

IM processes for finished goods generally revolve around the use life cycle phase. The IM processes work from the back end, that is the volume of finished goods in the pipeline and at distributors, including consumer stores, is based on the expected demand. Once expected demand for the given time period, say a week, at a location is established then IM processes focus on knowing the volume at the location. The volume on hand at the location is reported and analyzed using pre-established algorithms to identify variances.

The IM variance analysis process determines when the volume on hand, in transit, and expected production is at, below, or over target. Of course this information is likely to be rapidly changing so speed is important. When variances exceed thresholds established by IM analysis then failure modes are identified. Rapid communication of the failure modes to the appropriate organizations within the entity are critical IM functions. When this is done well this is the key value proposition for the IM PRMS processes for finished goods.

CHAPTER 8 – HIGHLIGHTS

- **Historical**

- **Functional**

- **Customer**

Founded in the past and continuing in the current world of PRM a significant weakness is found in the organizational and integration relationships of PRMS. This condition was created by the way that PRMS has evolved over time. As entities have grown in complexity and size PRM has become more critical. In the 21st century the field of management in general has become a recognized discipline and accepted field. This field really came into it's own in the mid 1950's and was rapidly accepted across industry, academia, and government organizations. As management grew and improved "systems" became the thing.

The management field and associated systems did not include PRMS as a discrete area, rather as several areas. Often these areas were not integrated and for many reasons no advantage to integration was evident. The PRMS is not an organization, it is a system, and generally there does not need to be one organization that executes all the elements of the system. There are several good approaches to organizational execution of PRMS, but one method stands out.

The best method identified to date is to align the logistics, inventory management, and physical distribution organizations to execute PRMS. One developing approach for doing this is to centralize these activities around and in the supply chain organization of an entity to execute the entities PRMS. This is not the only way, but it is superior to other options. Some organizations have moved this way as they recognized that the advantage of not ending the supply chain upon receipt of items, but rather carrying through the strengths of the supply chain to include PRMS.

PRMS functions have been around a long time, but there was a distinct event that changed how these things were done in the United States, and then throughout the industrial world. This event was precipitated by the after effects of World War II. President Truman had identified problems with the management of the huge amount of surplus PR left from the war. He sent a special message to the congress on March 5, 1948. The subject of the message was "The Need for a Modern System for the Management of Government Property". The first paragraph of President Truman's message summarized the issues and the approach very well:

"In accordance with the Government's settled policy of eliminating temporary war agencies as soon as practicable, I recommend that the Congress now provide for the liquidation of the temporary arrangements for disposing of surplus war propety and for the completion of the remaining disposal activities within the permanent Federal establishment. At the same time, the Congress should provide for a number of improvements in the permanent system for the procurement, use and disposal of Government property. For a number of years the Federal Government has needed a better system of property management. The present arrangements, which have been developed under piecemeal legislation dating as far back as 1870, are inadequate to meet the present requirements of the Government. That legislation contains many obsolete provisions and does not provide for the central leadership and direction necessary to coordinate the complex activities concerned with the procurement, use and disposal of Government property".

At that time, and continuing today the US Federal Government is the single largest owner of PR of all types. The Congress reacted well to President Truman's message and passed the Federal Property and Administrative Services act of 1949, and has kept up the legislation over time. The Federal Government has done a great job of maintaining "our" (after all the tax payers are the real owners) PR. Even with all of the problems that we hear about, these problems really only affect a small percentage of the government's PR, say less than 2% on average.

While the Federal Government has done a great job managing PR, the organization of the PRM functions that was set up and then evolved over time is naturally very bureaucratic. Private entities can do better by emulating the systems but not the bureaucratic approach to organizing and executing the systems. The PRM relationship to other disciplines and related system was described in Chapter 4 – Interrelated Disciplines.

To move PRM organizations and functions from process oriented areas to a key part of entity management systems requires a shift to a value added producer orientation. This can be accomplished, in part, by focusing on improving PRM relationships. These improvements are based on the assumption that the PRM functions and processes are operating within acceptable performance parameters. When the PRM functions and processes are consistently operating within the acceptable parameters the work of focusing on relationships pays dividends and adds significant value to an entities PRMS.

Customer Relationships

As with other management systems within an entity the PRM has at least two classifications of customers. Internal customers depend on the PRMS for both products and services that these other organizations need to conduct their business. External customers also depend on the PRMS for products and services though it is likely that the needs of external customers are predominately indirect through other organizations. The recognition of the importance of these customer relationships by the organizations chartered with the PRMS functionality is critical for the success of an entities PRM.

Internal customers need information about PR so they can do their jobs. A simple, but clear example of this is the need for janitors to have toilet paper for the restrooms. The toilet paper is a critical commodity and must be available for the janitors to do their jobs putting the paper in the restrooms. The PRMS provides the information to the janitorial staff of where this critical commodity is located, or when it's due to their location so that they have what the need. When the janitors do their job this in turn enables organizations that need restrooms to do their work to complete their missions. While simple and somewhat tongue in cheek this example demonstrates that PRM delivers either services, or products (the TP), either in physical form or information to internal customers.

Many current organizations that execute PRMS do not recognize the importance of identifying and meeting their internal customer needs. These organizations don't allocate resources necessary to handle internal customers which results in contentious relationships and disconnects that cost the entity in both productivity and cost as the ignored internal customers do something to meet their needs. Often this results in internal organizations doing their own PRMS work and this is usually not the most efficient way to do business, but this happens because the PRMS implementing organization did not recognize and meet their internal customer's needs. This condition creates multiple nonintegrated processes which result in more costly PRMS work.

PRMS implementing organizations that do not focus on external customer needs create significant risk for the entities sustainability for the work being done for their customers. Examples of products and services provided by PRMS for external customers are information, generally reports of PR held or other information needed by the clients, or delivery of PR to the customer for them to perform their work. When PRMS implementing organizations do not deliver the products and services other organizations step in and create less than efficient processes to deliver products & services to clients.

The fix to the problem of PRMS implementing organizations failure to meet customer needs is to address the problem directly. PRMS processes must include methods to identify the customer set and then implement activities to meet the customer's needs. This requires that the functions that are PRM implementing organizations do things differently than they have in the past. Since the late 1980s and early 1990s PRM implementing organizations have conducted "customer satisfaction surveys"; this approach does not identify internal or external customer needs, rather it measures how well these PRM functions perform what they believe their jobs are. The new approach to move into the best classes of PRMS is to ask internal and external customers, and surveys may be a tool for this, what they need and want. Then when the PRMS implementing organizations have figured out what they need to do to satisfy customer needs, they should test how well this mission is performed.

This new approach will be resisted by many PRM implementing organizations because of things like, not enough time or money and protests that they must do some basic things whether other organization's like it or not. While these barriers are likely in place the true best in class PRM leaders will figure out how to overcome the barriers necessary to identify and meet internal and external customer needs.

CHAPTER 9 – HIGHLIGHTS

- **Value Chain**

- **Case**

- **Costs**

The value chain for PRM has interfaces with virtually all of an entity's activities. PRM is an enterprise-wide process and the value added is significant when the work is organized and managed well. Specific value is added within the operations of an enterprise through executing a well organized and implemented PRM system. When organizations that implement PRMS complete a strategy plan for each classification of PR this results in lower costs to the entity across the entire life cycle. These lower costs ultimately pay dividends through the ability of the entity to invest the delta costs in other activities.

The best example of how implementing organized and efficient PRM provides value is the Walmart story. and specifically in contrast to the Kmart story. Both Walmart and Kmart opened their first stores in 1962. Kmart's first store was opened in Garden City, Michigan while Walmart's first store was opened in Rogers, Arkansas. Kmart used normal standard PRM processes and systems and by the turn of the century reported $37.1 billion in annual revenue. Walmart pioneered leading edge PRM processes and systems and reported $205 billion in annual revenue at the turn of the century and has continued to grow and is the world's largest retailer. Kmart struggled early in the 21st century and continues to fall behind Walmart today. The difference, proven in many case studies, is the way that Walmart operated their PRM systems. Walmart developed processes and tools to keep track of PR, especially the inventory and supply chain processes that they used to acquire and management items sold in stores and replenish on time resulting in lower inventory and carrying costs. Moreover the PRMS interfacing activities, especially logistics and distribution, were integrated with sales and merchandising activities.

The total cost of managing the PR of an entity does not leap out at you in most financial statements or budgets. Many agencies and companies only consider the cost of PRM to be the costs of the organization or organizations that are responsible for some elements of PRM. For example, requirement identification, purchasing, receiving, distribution, inventory management, PR control, and PR disposal or reinvestment, and so on. It is true that these are traditionally considered the cost of managing PR; it is not true that these costs accurately represent the total cost of managing and entities PR.

PRMS Costs

The total cost of managing the PR that an entity must have to perform its mission is actually comprised of several key elements that encompass much more than the cost of the organizations that provide management services. Key elements of total cost are based on understanding that the users of the PR spend time and other resources in managing the physical assets that they use. The PR users cost comprise much more of the total cost than the organizations that provide management services and systems. These user borne costs are not usually considered as part of PRM costs, but are often a major element of the true costs. As shown in the Walmart example, PRM processes and systems impacts can drive costs up or down across the entire enterprise. The cost impacts can be either as discrete physical asset cost or as labor costs across the entity as organizations struggle to complete their missions with less than adequate physical asset support or through duplication of effort as multiple organizations do the same work.

There is a proven cost model that can be used to identify the total cost of PRM and also to quantify the value added through PRMS. The model is fairly simple but requires a significant amount of data collection to operate. It is important to do the work to collect the date commensurate with the size of the PRMS so that the true costs and value are demonstrable by PRMS implementing organizations. The PRMS total cost model uses key elements and parametric estimates in combination to identify costs and values. This cost model can be used by any size organization as it uses information that is readily available through data collection and is then synthesized using organizational specific parameters.

The cost model is operated by determining the costs for three overarching activities by estimating or using actual costs for three sub-elements of cost and then using a standard ratio to identify where costs are compared to best in class and to determine value added factors for PRMS. The elements of the total cost model for an enterprise wide PRM are:

- PRM systems implementing organizations labor
- PRM system tools – the PR used to implement PRMS
- PRMS User-Field costs

The sub-elements of costs are identified in table 9.1 below.

Elements	Sub-elements					
PRMS Labor	Requirement Identification	Procurement	Logistics & Distribution	Utilization Support	Inventory Mgmt	Disposal
PRMS Tools	Procedures	Automated Systems	Facility Mgmt	Maintenance and Repairs		
PRMS Users	Interface with PRM Organizations	Interface with automated systems	Physical Verification			

Table 9.1 – PRMS Cost Model Elements and Sub-elements

The sub-elements costs are identified and summed to determine the primary cost element values. The model can be customized to meet the specific needs of any entity and then when synthesized with the cost value ratios the total cost and value of PRMS for the enterprise can be quantified and compared.

Physical Resource Management

The ratios for identification of cost and value are:

- PRMS Cost / Total Enterprise Cost: measures the proportion of an organization's total costs that are PRMS prime costs. The benchmark for value is based on historical costs compared to current costs. PRMS value is the delta between historical costs and current costs.

- PRMS Cost / Total Enterprise Revenue: measures the proportion of an organization's revenue that are PRMS cost. The benchmark for value is based on historical costs compared revenue and current PRMS cost compared to revenue. PRMS value is the delta between historical costs and current costs.

CHAPTER 10 – HIGHLIGHTS

- **Risks & Liabilities**

- **Performance Evaluation**

- **Stockholder/Stakeholder Value**

There is no secret to good leadership, it's just plain hard work. As in other management disciplines there are techniques to developing and implementing PRM. A key aspect of this is leadership, and this aspect is often overlooked in PRM. Often a practitioner is elevated to the leadership ranks because the individual is a good technician. Many times this works, but only after the good technician learns leadership and management, either through the school of hard knocks or through leadership development. A better approach is to elevate a leader who can master the functions or to provide leadership development to technicians and elevate those that can effectively lead the functions. Putting it all together requires forethought and basic activities like succession planning to have PRM leaders that deliver value to the entity.

Leadership of the PRMS requires that the basic skills of leadership be blended with understanding of the fundamentals of resource management, and these must be used to develop a function that focuses on delivery of value to the system stakeholders. There are three key aspects of leadership that, when blended together with the other usual leadership traits, result in outstanding leadership of the PRM system. These key aspects are:

- Risks & Liabilities Analysis
- Performance Evaluation
- Stockholder/Stakeholder Value

Risks & Liabilities

Leading the PRM system for any entity requires clear analysis of risks and liabilities. Decisions made about how PR are managed have enterprise level impacts and the ability of the PRMS leaders to identify risks and liabilities is critical. Then after identification of these risks and liabilities the analysis of the impacts the development of mitigation processes is a key aspect of managing PRM.

Risk Identification and Analysis

The PRM system must include processes that identify risks and then analyze the impacts. This is key to developing and implementing functions and processes that address the potential impacts to mitigate the risks. There are many methods and books out there on how to do risk management, so this section is not intended to provide details on how to do risk identification and analysis; rather it provides information on likely areas of potential risk and simple explanations of relevant areas of risk management. The best reason to be sure that the PRMS has risk functions and processes is that it is likely that no other element of an entity's management systems is likely to consider these areas in an integrated fashion. This results in sub-optimization of resource deployment to mitigate resource management risks.

A simple way to identify risks is to analyze the life cycle elements and identify risks that pose potential impact to either entity mission performance or financial performance. The table on the next page, Table 10-1, shows likely examples of risk areas for each PRM life cycle element (Requirement Identification, Acquisition, Asset Identification, Use, and Disposal).

Life Cycle Element	Mission Performance Risk	Financial Performance Risk
Requirement Identification	• Planning failures lead to shortages • Faulty requirements lead to erroneous usage applications	• Lack of requirement identification leads to increased costs • Requirement identification failures significantly increase life cycle costs
Acquisition	• Procurement lead time too long • Errors in correct sourcing • Errors in correct item	• Procurement costs too high • Errors require rework increasing cost
Asset Identification	• Failure to track • Availability problems • High asset volumes due to duplicates	• Failures increase acquisition costs • Failures increase carrying costs • Impact to asset valuations
Use	• Mission impact due to unavailability • Mission impact due to low utilization • Mission impact from low space utilization	• Failures increase processing costs • Failures increase carrying costs • Accounting problems
Disposal	• Continued use of outdated items • Clutter of operational areas • Safety & environmental problems	• Failure to achieve appropriate return on investment

Table 10-1 Life Cycle Risk Areas

Performance Evaluation

Evaluation of performance is a critical function for any entity-wide management system. Most people are familiar with annual, or more frequent, audits performed by outside firms of the books of publicly held corporations. These audits are an effective method of the performance of the financial systems of such entities. There are similar outside methods of audits that are available from consulting firms for an entities PRMS. These outside consultant activities are not well defined or accepted and therefore are rarely used with a primary reason for that being the high cost compared to derived value of such actions.

Another and probably more effective method for most organizations is to develop internal assessment processes for the PRMS. This is actually fairly easy to do using benchmark metrics that can be compared to metrics similar to the ratios for utilization discussed in Chapter seven. In addition to the metrics in Chapter seven there are a few metrics that measure the performance of the PRMS.

There are three key metrics that can be compared to benchmarks established by such organizations as the ASTM and others.

These metrics and typical benchmarks are described below:

Income / PRMS Cost: describes how efficiently the PRMS manages PR. Generally all elements of PRMS should have a cost ration between .05 and .09 of gross income.

Physical Resource Visibility and Accuracy/ Total PR: this is the true effectiveness of physical inventory actions. Generally an entity should have an item and value accuracy from physical inventories between 95% and 98% to have a low risk of impacting mission accomplishment.

Physical Resource Availability / Total Requests: when an organization has determined to store resources it should expect that demands produce the required resource between 98% and 99% of the time to have a low risk of impacting mission accomplishment.

There are other key metrics that should be used based on the unique needs of each entity. The primary focus is that such metrics become imbedded in PRMS operations to ensure continuous value to the mission accomplishment of the entity. The metrics should measure effectiveness of the PRMS in meeting the overall mission and not just the internal operation of the PRMS.

Stockholder/Stakeholder Value

PRMS leadership must have a continuing focus on the entity's highest level missions. This is critical because if the focus is on PRMS performance it can, and has often resulted in sub-optimization of the overall PRMS. I like to call this the "green eyeshade" syndrome. Many people are familiar with the denigrating term "bean counters" applied to accountants. Both the "green eyeshade" and "bean counter" labels are derived long term tendencies to sub-optimize support functions resulting in less than effective mission support.

Leadership of the PRMS must learn and communicate to the staff performing PRMS work the highest level missions of the entity. Continuous focus on the integration of PRMS with the mission outcomes must be maintained and always be the PRMS focus. Success for the PRMS must be linked to the mission outcomes vice internal PRMS processes.

The National Aeronautics and Space Administration (NASA) has been a leader in integrating functional support areas, including PRMS functions, with mission accomplishment for many years. An example of this is the use of astronauts to provide encouragement, including personal visits and awards to federal and contractor staff in the manned space program. At the Kennedy Space Center (KSC) during the early 1990s Astronauts delivered awards to the personnel that worked in the logistics warehousing facility. The awards ceremonies included the astronauts riding in forklifts that were used in the high bay storage areas. The astronauts expressed gratitude to the warehouse work force and were genuinely impressed with the work they did. This process very effectively linked the people in the PRMS to the people that "they" sent into space. The integration effect of this type of activity lasted for years. Leaders in PRMS will find ways to link their functions, processes, and people to the mission accomplishment of their organizations.

Leaders of the PRM function that can engage the people involved, in a way that makes them all feel like leaders, will bring about changes that improve the discipline of physical resource management. These changes will result in increased visibility of PRM in the executive management arena. While already considered an important activity by most businesses, the activities that comprise the current discipline of physical resource management are not usually integrated to deliver the best value for entities.

When physical resource management is set up with the best organization and implements the systems and processes in an integrated way, as described in this book, the discipline of PRM will demonstrate increased value to the enterprise.

Index

Index

Index

Index

Index

About Skybow Group

Skybow Group (SBG) provides writing & publishing services

You can contact SBG at Skybow.net or at Skybow@cableone.net

CPSIA information can be obtained at www.ICGtesting.com
Printed in the USA
LVOW06*1522050614

388780LV00006B/52/P